The
FLYING
GARCIAS

The
FLYING
GARCIAS

Richard Garcia

University of Pittsburgh Press

Pittsburgh • London

The publication of this book is supported by grants from the
National Endowment for the Arts in Washington, D.C., a Federal
agency, and the Pennsylvania Council on the Arts.

Published by the University of Pittsburgh Press, Pittsburgh, Pa.
15260
Copyright © 1993, Richard Garcia
Manufactured in the United States of America
Printed on acid-free paper

Library of Congress Cataloging-in-Publication Data

García, Richard, 1941–
    The flying Garcias / Richard Garcia.
       p.   cm.—(Pitt poetry series)
    ISBN 0-8229-3745-X (hard : alk. paper.—ISBN 0-8229-5499-0
(pbk. : alk. paper)
    I. Title. II. Series.
PS3557.A71122F57   1993
811'.54—dc20   92-50824
                                                                   CIP

A CIP catalogue record for this book is available from the British Library.
Eurospan, London

The author and publisher wish to express their grateful acknowledgment to
the following publications in which some of these poems first appeared:
Americas Review ("Waking to the Radio"); *Bilingual Review* ("Dixit
Dominus, Domino Meo"); *Bloomsbury Review* ("Held at Gunpoint, I
Remember the Fourth Grade"); *5 AM* ("Some Mornings," "Thing"); *Five
Fingers Review* ("The Death of Zorro," "Shadow Captain"); *The
Guadalupe Review* ("Sideways Angel," "Wide Awake at 3:30 A.M."); *The
Gettysburg Review* ("While Trading Clothes in a Rest Stop Bathroom");
Imagine ("The Contras," "Eternal Return"); *The Kenyon Review* ("Los
Amantes," "The Story of Keys"); *L.A. Weekly* ("My Life as a Dancer");
Mid-American Review ("The Book of Forgetting," "The Defiant Ones,"
"The Detective Gone Bad"); *North Dakota Quarterly* ("Pancho Villa in the
Land of Forever"); *OntheBus* ("A Good Year"); *Parnassus: Poetry in
Review* ("Mi Mamá, the Playgirl"); *Pearl* ("Like a Chicken About to Cross
a Road"); *Ploughshares* ("The Flying Garcias," "In the Year 1946," "Why I
Left the Church"); *Santa Monica Review* ("I Was a Teenage Zombie");
Seneca Review ("Pen," "Sadness and the Movies"); *Transfer Fifty* ("La
Calle del Niño Perdido," "Fish Grow as They Leave the Water"); *Tsunami*
("Chickens Everywhere"); and *Yellow Silk* ("Swinging from the Moon on a
Bosun's Chair").

The author wishes to thank the National Endowment for the Arts and the
California Arts Council for their generous support.

For Dinah

Contents

The
FLYING
GARCIAS

The Book of Dreams

If you dream of scissors,
two women, one light, one dark,
are whispering your name.

If you sit on the front stairs
at the bottom of the sea,
you are going to spend your life
waiting for someone.

If you are on your knees in the closet,
digging through a pile of shoes
you are going to learn something
you do not want to know.

"*Madre, dime,* what if I dream of the moon?"

"The moon is a woman, *Hijo,*
she comes, she goes,
she changes her mind.
She has power over women.
This will give her power over you."

The book of *One Thousand and One Dreams Explained*
is the only book in our house, and every word is true.
It's big, so big you have to climb a chair
and use both hands to lift the cover—

both hands turn the pages
that stretch out like wings.

La Calle del Niño Perdido

I find him, just an infant,
lying at the curb
playing with water, his brow
radiant with rain.

"Great," I say, "just what I need,
a baby." "Don't worry," he says,
"tiny as I am, I can speak,
and I know everything."

I carry him through the supermarket.
While I poke through grapefruit
he talks and talks,
sometimes in rhymed iambic pentameter,
telling me about his past lives,
transformations, famous battles,
and how the grapefruits remind him
of the asteroids
beyond Alpha Centauri.

We are interviewed on television.
He sits on my lap,
but will not say one word.
But I talk, my finger
strumming my lips, "blewrm, blewrm,
da da do, do," spittle
dribbles down my chin.

It is raining
on the Street of the Lost Child.
He rides my back
and whispers in my ear,

"Don't be sad,
I'll tell you a story."
Two bald men.
One very small.
Lost.

Shadow Captain

I am a little boy.
I live with two old people
who are my parents.
When I am bad
they chase me up the stairs.
But I am too fast for them.
I hide in the closet
thinking, "old, old, old."

Each night the shadows
of Messerschmitts and B-29s
slide across the wall of my room
with their tails flaming,
tracer bullets rise like fireflies
through dueling searchlights,
a cloud becomes a tornado
that spins like a mummy
unwinding its tape,
and each night my brother's shadow,
dressed in his captain's uniform,
untangles from all that smoke
and salutes me off to sleep.

Tonight is a special night.
I stay up to dance with the grown-ups.
We are a family that is famous
for our parties. We do *la raspa*,
weave a conga line, one-two-three
kick through all the rooms of our house.
At twelve o'clock there is an explosion
of tears, kisses, confetti, ornaments.
Walls fall away, backyard fences are flattened.

"Some party," my sister says, shaking her head
as everyone pokes through the wreckage.
My father has found his hula skirt and false teeth.
Cousin Robert has found his bongos.
But I just stand there looking up at the sky
dark with airplanes
returning in tight formation.
I am a little boy waking up at the end of the war
to see my brother's face
for the first time.

Why I Left the Church

Maybe it was
because the only time
I hit a baseball
it smashed the neon cross
on the church across
the street. Even
twenty-five years later
when I saw Father Harris
I would wonder
if he knew it was me.
Maybe it was the demon-stoked
rotisseries of purgatory
where we would roast
hundreds of years
for the smallest of sins.
Or was it the day
I wore my space helmet
to catechism? Clear plastic
with a red-and-white
inflatable rim.
Sister Mary Bernadette
pointed toward the door
and said, "Out! Come back
when you're ready."
I rose from my chair
and kept rising
toward the ceiling
while the children
screamed and Sister
kept crossing herself.
The last she saw of me
was my shoes disappearing
through cracked plaster.
I rose into the sky and beyond.

It is a good thing
I am wearing my helmet,
I thought as I floated
and turned in the blackness
and brightness of outer space,
my body cold on one side and hot
on the other. It would
have been very quiet
if my blood had not been
rumbling in my ears so loud.
I remember thinking,
Maybe I will come back
when I'm ready.
But I won't tell
the other children
what it was like.
I'll have to make something up.

Reflections of a Stowaway

A prim missionary lady. A down-and-out pilot. And me. A bumbling teenage stowaway hiding in a crate with a sad-eyed parrot, afraid of dreadful contaminations. I fondled my gun. It was the only thing that made me feel important.

The missionary was reading a book called *Reflections of Youth*. I liked the sound her nylons made as she crossed and uncrossed her legs.

I wanted to come out of hiding to tell her I would do anything, puncture tires for her if that was what she wanted.

And if we splashed down in the ocean I would spin around in my Mae West kicking sharks away from her. Even if all they really were doing was looking for affection.

Someday the pilot would sit in a bar in Panama, with the parrot on his shoulder, telling our story. No one would believe him. Any more than they believed the waitress when she claimed she had been posing as a voodoo priestess when she held up her father's general store.

In the Year 1946

In the year 1946 a young sailor came bounding up the stairs, leapt into the kitchen, and with his arms spread out, exclaimed, "I'm home!" We stared at him silently. Mother, brothers and sisters. But not his mother, brothers and sisters. "Sorry," he said, "wrong house."

I wonder what became of him? Is he still searching? Not so sprightly now, he drags himself up the stairs. People no longer leave their doors unlocked and he has to ring the bell. Each house looks almost like his house. Each astonished family almost like his family.

In the year 1946 we sat in the kitchen often, perhaps listening to the radio. I remember a certain moment when I, who had been such a good boy, felt possessed for the first time by a mad desire. I raised my head toward the ceiling, spat, and said, "That's for you God." Then I clasped my hands together, shook them above my head like a triumphant fighter, stared down at the floor and yelled, "Yeah Devil!"

I looked like a bird with a busted wing as my sister dragged me around the house in a hammerlock. We stopped before each picture of each saint where I had to apologize and kiss the glass.

My mother and father, two brothers and one sister sat in the kitchen as we made our rounds. Silent. They were wondering, Who is this boy? Where did he come from? Are we his family?

Mi Mamá, the Playgirl

When my mother left Mexico, soldiers commandeered the train, forcing the passengers to get off and wait for the next one. Later they passed it lying on its side, burning.

She wore black dresses. Her closet was lined with identical pairs of black shoes. She constantly advised me to jump off the bridge while the tide was going out.

Long after my father was dead, she complained that his side of the bed still sank down. "*Viejo*," she would tell him, "If you have somewhere to go, please go. At seventy, she went out to nightclubs. Twisted her knee doing the bunny hop. Talked for hours to forty-year-old lovers on the phone. My brothers were ashamed.

After she died, she came to see me as she had promised. My father came, too. We sat around in the kitchen drinking coffee as if nothing had happened. My father looked great, said he'd been working out. She stroked his forearm, smiling at his tattoo of the dancing hula girl. When they left it was nothing dramatic. They just walked out the door and up a street that seemed to reach into the night sky. How beautiful, I thought, as I was waking, the stars shining in my mother's hair.

Thing

If we could have seen it,
it would have looked like
a face that emerges
in cracked plaster
or patterns of linoleum
that seems to smile at you
and is never seen again.

Could we smell it?
Did it make a sound?
I don't know,
but we knew
when it was near
by a brief odor
of cut flowers
where there were none
or the way
the wind chimes
seemed to play the
opening notes
of a popular song.

If it had a shape,
it would have been
a shape made by the space
between us. That is why
when we lay on different
sides of the bed
the middle sank in.

We joked about it.
Named it Thing.
Although it was invisible,

we pretended to pet it,
stroking the air.

We would hurry home from work
just to be near it.
But it was getting too big
for our small apartment.
We wanted to go away,
to leave it behind.
But who would feed it?
Who would love it
as we had loved it?

Reception at the Yacht Club

The bride played saxophone.
She could really blow that thing.
Her feet firmly planted,
she stood in front of Charlie's band
in her white dress and veils.

The woman who made the cheesecake
looked like a cheesecake—
billowy and sad.
She had always loved the groom
and her tears, dry now,
plopped on her dress like powdered sugar.

Charlie played "When Irish Eyes Are Smiling."
I led my lover's sister across the polished floor.
"I haven't waltzed since high school," she said.
This is our last dance, I could have said, but didn't—

Instead, I nodded to her father's ghost.
He had made it to the wedding
as I knew he would, even with nothing to wear
but that hospital nightgown.

The music stopped, but I kept dancing
since I wouldn't be dancing here anymore.
Nobody knew, nobody but Charlie,
and he's the piano player at the Yacht Club.

He's seen it all, those guys
with the woman upstairs
and the woman downstairs
and nothing but a stairway in between.

Some Mornings

Some mornings you just don't know.
The coffee smells good.
You see clothing on the floor
and put it on. It fits.

But this shirt could be anyone's shirt
and you could be anyone.
A professor of arcane languages.
A dishwasher in a diner.
You could be several people
who don't even know each other.

Stop this. Have some coffee.
Place the ring on your finger,
the keys in your pocket.
The driver's license in the wallet
should give you enough to go on for now.

If people seem to know you,
respond as if you know them.
Don't worry about it. Wait in the room.
Soon a woman will come through the door.
Her arms will be full of flowers.
She will explain everything.

Watching a French Movie
with Hebrew Subtitles

The young woman is a guest on his island,
or a hostage, his niece, or his charge.
He—silver-haired, courtly,
but with a scar across his cheek
that hints at a violent past—is a pirate,
or a kindly uncle. Whichever, he treats her well,
lets her wander through his big house,
through the library with the leather-bound editions,
red velvet chairs draped with Spanish lace.

He never opens the mail that piles up in the foyer.
One night she wakes, startled out of a dream,
and overhears a quarrel at the front gate
that ends with a cry and a moan.
And the string quartet that plays for their dinner—
are they captives?

He persuades her to pose for him
standing beneath the figurehead of his ship
holding two conch shells
while he paints her portrait.
I recognize the word *ima*, mother.
Sometimes, when she wanders the cliffs alone,
she turns and sees him in the distance,
as if he were guarding her.

It is hot, humid. She can't sleep.
She hears drums, follows them to the slave quarters
where he sits, staring at darkness,
while a creole woman, naked from the waist up,
dances in firelight.

Next day his workmen call her to come see
what they have found. A statue of a woman without arms
buried in the sand. The figure has a child's face,
but the body seems older, voluptuous.
The workmen point to the statue and then to her,
exclaiming, *"C'est vous! C'est vous!"*
He kneels in the pit, looking up at her, brushing wet sand
from the throat and shoulders.

Fish Grow as They Leave the Water

Paul's fish burrowed in the garden, leaving mounds of over-turned earth. Red fish heads hung from branches.

Dennis's fish stared at us sideways as we swam with them through a pond, their lips puffed for a kiss.

Nash's fish made the pathetic squeaking sound carp make as they are fried alive, their heads held tenderly out of oil with chopsticks.

I followed the Garcia River—under freeways and scaffolds, through a cafeteria, into a locker room, where it squeezed out of a ventilator and into a parking lot. Here it was just a puddle. Who would guess that this was the source of a mighty river? I squatted and waited.

Waited so long the puddle became a lake of gray dust that shimmered just like real water. Casting a number 10 silver ghost, I caught that rare bonefish that swims fossil-like, through solid stone.

Well, almost caught it. It disappeared in the depths, about to swallow the skeleton of a smaller fish that was about to swallow the skeleton of a smaller fish.

Like a Chicken About to Cross a Road

She hates the way I chop chicken, letting the cleaver fall where it may. "Mangled," she calls it.

I hate the way she cooks chicken. I sit across from her trying to chew. "This chicken died fighting," I say. "They had to shoot this chicken."

What's wrong with me? Sometimes when we kiss I smell raw chicken. I dream I am a parachutist crashing through a chicken coop, or that I step barefoot over piles of plucked chickens.

I remember my father killing that chicken in the kitchen. It got loose. Even without a head, it ran around the room spasmodically flapping, spurting blood on the walls.

"Forget the chickens," she says, "come to bed." Should I sleep? Nestle next to her? Would she wake? What kind of dreams would she have if I whispered in her ear, The sky is falling?

Chickens Everywhere

You can't escape chickens. Chickens are all the rage. Alone in your car, you turn on the radio. It's The Chickens singing Glenn Miller's "In the Mood."

Even in your sleep there's no escape. You dream of a woman. She comes toward you opening her bathrobe. Between her legs, a chicken peeks out.

You are in the yard staring at your chicken. Your chicken is staring at you. Your chicken grows until it is six feet tall. You embrace. Never have you felt pleasure like this. You wake straddling your pillow.

You go to see your lady friend. She is wearing feathers. She moves her neck from side to side and clucks. It's no use. Walk alone in the night. Keep your collar up and your head down. The night is a chicken with enormous black wings. And you, little one, are a grain of wheat on the floor of a barn.

Sideways Angel

My wife gave me a book to read, an account
of my life starting a few days after my death.
It began with a test: I had to walk three times
around the block—the first not stepping on cracks,
the second avoiding the spaces, the third, which was the hardest,
stepping only on chalk smudges.

This accomplished, some official-looking men
slipped their hands under my scapulas and pulled my wings out.
Something was wrong, which seemed to amuse them.
Oh, I would be able to fly all right, but not very high, and only
      sideways.

Sideways, only sideways, without much control,
bumping into buildings, utility poles.
At least I wasn't solid. With a little effort,
I could pass through them.

I floated in the wind above an open pit mine.
Down below me, men shuffled slowly back and forth like prisoners.
One of them looked up, squinted
as if he could see me, and smiled.
As I flew off he said, "Look, there's a smudge
on my glasses that looks like an angel."

Sideways only sideways, slipping through slanted rain
without getting wet. Sideways avoiding the cracks,
spaces, and smeared labyrinths of hopscotch.
Sideways, all profile, always slipping off to the side
of my afterlife like a striped-faced jackal, sideways.

While Trading Clothes in a Rest Stop Bathroom

Do you think it odd that my body
should suffer
a sea change
every seven years or so?

Wherever I go
I leave a trail an experienced tracker
can follow. Even through water
he sees pebbles disturbed
in the shape of my shoes,
or a drop of blood
on a sharp edge of rust-colored shale.

I have altered my voice, my hair, my flesh,
even edited old photographs,
cutting my face out—erased my name
from hotel ledgers.

If captured I shall deny
all knowledge of my existence.
I will insist, even if I no longer
have a body, I am not the same person
that danced in those tattletale bones.

Not me. What am I anyway?
Just voices, just a name,
an alias written on scarred enamel.
You might as well go out on the highway,
lean into the wind, and ask a dust devil
to show its passport and papers.

Fly Fishing in England

I expected this famous stream
would be a landscape by Constable—one corner
of the sky piled with clouds, farmhouse in the distance.
But it was more like a drainage ditch,
and I was irritated with the rules: no nymphs,
dry flies only, cast upstream.

I turned in disgust from the cement-lined water
stocked with fat hatchery trout. Turned away
from the tangled reflections in the current
and thoughts of the money it had cost
to secure a beat on this river.

Then I saw him, John Donne, sitting beneath an oak,
his fly rod leaning in the crook of a branch.
He motioned for me to sit beside him.
I walked over and lowered myself slowly.
Sit, sit, he said, patting the grass hard,
as if to assure me it was real.

We spoke of his buddy Isaac Walton.
A lousy fisherman! Donne said. Many a time
I was having a great day, standing in the stream
killing 'em and Walton sat on the bank
throwing pebbles in the water just to ruin my fishing!

John, I said, the woman in your poem "The Baite"—
was she real? A beauty, he said, She was the abbess
of nearby convent—and quite a fisherwoman too.
A sly one, she would pretend to be out for a walk,
her rod disguised as a staff.

Once I followed her to her spot and hid in the bushes.
Her fly, a gray bloa, lightly hackled with a feather
from a tomtit's tail, got caught in a sunken log.
She slipped out of her habit, stripped off her undergarments
and waded in after it. I became a school of little fishies
that swam around her legs, between her thighs.

Then he turned and strode away from the concrete embankment
and entered the well-worn fisherman's path
that wove through brush. He called out to me to follow—
but I stayed put. There have been many times
when I thought a river spoke my name.

Glass

Glass is what happens
when lighting strikes sand.
Construction workers
carrying large panes of glass
through stopped traffic
are often mistaken
for a procession of statues.

Walking at dusk, when windows reflect
an orange sky, I want to enter
the steamy kitchens without being seen,
to sit surrounded by conversation
and the clatter of dishes.

"What is glass?" I once asked my mother.
"Air," she answered, "air that becomes hard."

I spent my first days of life in a glass box.
A nurse would appear, slip her hand
into a rubber glove that dangled over me
and wiggle her fingers, trying to make me smile.
I would turn my head away from her
and touch the cool, hard glass.

Sometimes when walking,
I stop for no reason, as if I felt glass
pressed against my forehead,
as if I heard my mother's fingers
drum against the window,
the approach of a distant army,
horses galloping
along beaches turned to glass.

Pen

Taken apart
in the back
of a paddy wagon,
you can use it
to open handcuffs.

When you lose it
it goes to that place
in your mind
with all the other
lost things—

the valley of keys,
the tree of single socks,
depository of loaned books,
the forgotten ones
torn away from their names.

But nobody ever loses hope.
Even digging your own grave
while your executioners
stand around smoking,
you think maybe it is a joke
or a test of some kind.

Losing a pen
allows you to find it.
Standing by a stream
you see it bobbing toward you
like a little boat.
It speaks
but only to those other pens
that have also lost their way
and returned.

Dixit Dominus, Domino Meo

He insists that I play dominoes with him. I don't know how. But I shouldn't be afraid. He is a kindly man, distinguished looking in his uniform. We have long talks about Rilke, Beethoven's last quartets. He has read my poetry. "How I envy you poets," he sighs.

He shrugs off my escape attempts. When they bring me back, he just shakes his head. "It's the snow," I tell him. If it is summer, I blame the villagers who march behind me with their pitchforks. "What's the use of escaping," I say, "when the whole world is a prison?"

"Write a poem about it," he says.

We sit, and with infinite patience, he instructs me in the deadly language of dominoes: Snake eyes. Bleeding. Boxcars. Boneyard. Ivory soap.

My Life as a Dancer

I have danced between collapsing skylines
of dirty dishes. I have danced
folded in fetal position
under a suitcase in an apple orchard.
I have danced for the police,
nimble, keeping my feet between kicks and punches.

I have danced with fragrant evening gowns
while hiding in closets.
Danced with shadows that had no reflection.
Danced through plate glass
with a half-naked woman slung over one shoulder.
Danced in moonlight with a slender-waisted broom.

Every man has his own dance.
The traffic cop does his scarecrow style.
The black man with rags for shoes dances
with arms akimbo while worshiping a power pole.
The window washer forty stories up does his
polishing the sky to a high luster.
The custodian, members of the board,
mail room clerk, form a line that snakes
down the emergency stairwell
into the parking lot of the supermarket.

Mine goes like this—a kind of bouncing,
herky-jerky, bobbing hanged man,
semen-dripping dance.
If you ask me what it's called
I may not answer you. I may say,
Don't bother me, can't you see I'm dancing?

Doing the Tarantella with Lola Montez

Using their webs like sails, spiders rise
into the stratosphere.
Their webs stick to other webs
forming clouds, whispy mare's tails
that twist across the sky.
When they get too heavy,
they fall back to earth
in silvery clumps
that frighten school children.

Some women make love like spiders.
With their tongues they cover you
in thin webs of pleasure.

Nothing can make you so sad
as the bite of certain tarantulas.
You can die from sadness.
Only frantic dancing can save you.
People who see you
start dancing too—
as if they were tied
to invisible strings.

But I am the happiest of all.
I have danced with Lola Montez,
Queen of the Barbary Coast,
who stamped her heels
on the floorboards
at the small rubber spiders
that bounced beneath her dress.

Sadness and the Movies

Sometimes you take it personal.
The pressure of the wind
against your eyes that feels like crying.
The sign on the road
that says Go Back
You Are Going The Wrong Way.
The automatic doors
of the Alpha Beta
that open for everyone
but you. The old ladies
pushing grocery carts into your hip,
and their little snapping dogs,
Pekinese and Lhasa apsos.

Like the sad part
of the movies—some suffering
in the beginning and middle, everything
and everyone against you,
as you are surrounded by infidel hordes
who want to brandish your head on a spear.
They are coming again in the morning.
You have saved a bullet for yourself.

When suddenly you hear them,
the bagpipes, echoing
from a mountain pass—
The Royal Scots Dragoon Guards,
marching in their kilts
playing their version of "Amazing Grace."
And you are Yojimbo
when he gets his sword back
slicing the air into fifty pieces.

Like the end of *Zulu*.
You accept your fate.
It is as good a day to die as any.
Thousands of warriors
line the crest of the hills
for their final charge.
Raising their spears and shields in the air
they salute you—and still chanting the lion chant
that sounds like some enormous unstoppable machinery,
they turn away from your smoking outpost
and march toward their villages,
their poets improvising songs about your courage,
your crazy, crazy courage.

Eternal Return

The older prisoners
wanted the gun carved from soap
painted black with shoe polish.
The younger prisoners wanted to tunnel out
like Charles Bronson in *The Great Escape*.
Or to float away on a raft
made of raincoats and rubber cement,
like Clint Eastwood in *Escape from Alcatraz*.
The guards heard the prisoners escaping
but waited to see the end of a movie
in which prisoners escaped
while the guards watched a movie
in which the prisoners were escaping
while the guards watched a movie
about prisoners escaping.
Some of the guards wanted to be Nazis—
blond, handsome, malevolent.
Others—a Mexican posse
with sombreros, bandoleers, mustaches,
shooting their pistols in the air.
The prisoners had fled across the Badlands in circles.
The guards pursued in circles.
After what seemed a decent interval,
guards and prisoners converged in an open field
and traded clothes.
The prisoners, now the guards,
marched their captives through small towns,
where silent crowds lined the streets.
The guards were proud—slapping each other on the back,
spit-polishing shiny buttons with their sleeves.
The prisoners dragged their feet and muttered among themselves.
Already they were planning their escape.

A Good Year

It is a good year for midgets, 1939.
We see them on the move,
buses stuffed with little people
belonging to rival families and circuses,
mooning each other through the windows
as they race down highways
toward California and the yellow brick road.

They fondle chorus girls in hallways,
fight with knives in dressing rooms,
get so drunk they fall into toilets.
And long after midnight,
regiments of studio cops are seen
stumbling from the seedier neighborhoods,
a passed-out munchkin hanging limp
under each arm.

This is the year
Mr. Smith goes to Washington
to stand up for the little guy,
the year the little people
are dressed like soldiers in camouflage
with leaves and twigs on their hats.
When they lower their heads to sleep
they become a field of ivy.

As the year ends we see some of them
coasting along a back road in Florida
in a beat-up bus that is out of gas.
They have spent all their money on whores.
They are arguing in German. Finally they agree.
Wherever the bus stops they will build their town.
The houses, street lamps, mail boxes, everything, will be small.

I Was a Teenage Zombie

It makes my teachers angry
to have a dead person in class.
There are three of us now.
We are the stars of the basketball team.
Not very coordinated as we stumble
across the court, but we never tire.
"Not fair," the other players say,
and take up a petition.

The three of us have decided—
we shall not attend our funerals.
We are expelled from school but that's OK.
We have found a book of instructions
by a seventeenth-century pirate zombie.
As we leave to found our own republic
my lover waves good-bye from the school yard.
I don't recall being in school with her,
but dreams are like that.
I will come back for her someday
when I have learned how to live.
Already I have read all of chapter one.
It is called "How Zombies Cry."

The Death of Zorro

Cisco and Pancho ride into the sunset,
their high-pitched laughter echoing through canyons.
Of course, we know who they really are
by the way the secret service follows
at a discreet distance, pretending to be
the wagon train from "Death Valley Days."
The assassin gallops
along the edge of the Sierra Nevada,
his cape flapping in the red air.
Will Sergeant Garcia
find the black panties
that have been used as a mask?
Will he sniff their aristocratic perfume
of jasmine and bougainvillea?
Will he arrive,
waving the panties in the air,
in time to warn the president?
Everything has been arranged.
The assassin will be assassinated.
Sergeant Garcia will don the cape
and ride crisscross along the border
leaving a trail of incriminating Zs
resembling stitches across a wound.

Pancho Villa in the Land of Forever

It gets so crowded in eternity
that time is all mixed up.
When Columbus bumps into America
the Pilgrims appear.

They don't like the trees, so dark
and looming, and begin to chop them down—
making space for explorers and mounted conquistadors
who clank around in their armor like creatures
half machine, half animal.

Now there is room for the pioneers
who arrive out of breath, plant grass,
then lean on their rifles and hatchets
and sing, "Green Grows the Grass."

Pancho Villa and his men are hiding in the shadows.
They scratch their heads and wonder,
What are these gringos they always sing about?
Pancho Villa strides into the light
dragging his bright spurs. "Hey, gringos,"

he shouts, "you can't camp here, it is forbidden."
But they ignore him. Already they have invented cement
and are busy burying the grass.
"Go away," says one of the gringos to Pancho Villa,
"you don't even have a badge."

So the Mexicans ride off
in a cloud of dust and *ay yi yi*'s.
Tonight is the night they cross the border
and raid Columbus, New Mexico,
where they torch the skeletal remains
of the Niña, the Pinta and the Santa María.

Waking to the Radio

If I yawn, traffic slows.
If I cough,
stockbrokers fall off the ladders
that lean against my ribs.
I am the morning news.
I am the president

whose raspy voice clatters
like an armored personnel carrier
full of bouncing militia.
It is winter and my chest is stuffed
with frozen derelicts and postmen.

My waist is in Central America
where intestines are strung across trees
like Christmas lights.
It is dark there
and vans cruise the narrow streets
of my veins, their headlights
sniffing doors that lie down
in their own shadows
pretending to be coffins.

Is it my backbone that emerges
from a plastic bag? My foot
that swings from the mouth of a dog?

Through the pillow I hear the tape-recorded
voice of the secretary
who hides under her desk
and whispers into the phone
while a jealous husband
stalks through the office
with a pump-action shotgun.

The Defiant Ones

Two convicts shackled on a chain,
running across a field—
one a romantic
the other a classicist.
The romantic
wants to run toward a farmhouse
where he is sure
the farmer's lovely daughter
will find them hiding in the barn
and bring oatmeal and a file.
Two convicts on a chain running across a field—
one an ex-marine turned pacifist,
the other a pacifist
convicted of double murder.
Both are in agreement
neither of them shall ever reveal
they were Siamese twins
separated at birth.
Two convicts on a chain—
one a rich fop
with an accent like Leslie Howard
in *The Scarlet Pimpernel.*
"Well, sink me," he says
as they wade chin deep
through the swamp, "I do believe
my breeches shall be dreadfully damp."
The other a tattooed language poet
from East L.A. who alienated the jury
by reading a six-page poem
that consisted only of commas.
Two convicts on a chain—
not Tony Curtis and Sidney Poitier,
but the remake, with Wallace Stevens
and Ernest Hemingway

punching, kicking, and gouging,
as they roll on the dusty
grease-stained, straw-strewn
floor of a freight car.
Two convicts shackled on a chain,
running across a field—
one black, one white, both blind,
stumbling, pulling against each other.
In the distance you hear the baying
of bloodhounds . . .

The Quiet Ones

When the bikers roar into town
gardeners shall lop the wings off topiary swans,
the barber will take his hairbrushes
out to the back alley and set them on fire,
and the young ladies of the Royal Academy
Finishing School will learn how to say
"There is no tomorrow" in French.
That is when the town librarian
shall hide naked in the basement stacks
between records of mining expeditions
and histories of the founding fathers.

The bikers will come at 10:35 A.M. on a Sunday
with figureheads they have scavenged
from the antique shops of six Western states
arched over their handlebars, and the furry straps
of their aviator caps frantically flapping.
They shall roar into town, not with a sequence
of unbaffled explosions,
but with a quiet, steady roar,
like the crunching and hissing approach
of an enormous glacier heard from a great distance.

They shall roar in so quietly
no one will notice
that the high school marching band
rattles elaborate paradiddles
against the skins of drums that make no sound.
No one will notice
the church bells
tolling no louder than a page turning.

Held at Gunpoint,
I Remember the Fourth Grade

While the gunman isn't paying much attention
I grab the letter opener
and begin to open the mail.
Nothing much—bills, a parking ticket,
appeals for money and an advertisement
for carpet cleaning with photographs
of missing children on the back.

While the gunman isn't paying much attention
I contemplate my rescue by a posse
of female warriors led by an Amazon queen.
The gunman and I will recognize each other
as victims of the same grammar school,
buddies often punished for our inattention.

While the gunman isn't paying much attention
I slip the letter opener into an envelope
I seem to have addressed to myself in another life.
I remember Miss Tucker's warning about the consequences
of poor penmanship. I remember her eyes
flashing across the pages where my sad alphabet
crawled like wounded soldiers under barbed wire.

The gunman, exasperated by my inattention,
leans the muzzle of his .45 against my forehead.
I would like to make the appropriate gesture of submission,
raise my arms—but I have lost the belt to my plaid bathrobe.
The gunman looks down at the floor, as if he had forgotten
what comes next, or as if lost in admiration
of the Goofy slippers that I bought at Disneyland.

A Hero in the War

The Japanese, aware that Americans have short memories and learn all their history from the movies, are buying up the Hollywood studios.

Gradually, they are changing the endings of World War II movies. Eventually the Americans will come to believe they lost the war.

A used car salesman wakes up with the night sweats and reaches for the gun he keeps by his bed. He was a hero in the war. Or was it a movie he saw?

Maybe he was a hero in the war and he wrote a book about it, then starred in a movie about his life. But he is confused. It seems the last time he saw the movie on late-night TV, he died.

He grabs his gun and runs outside screaming, "I am not dead!" But nobody in the neighborhood pays much attention to him.

Not at the all-night convenience store. Not the police who bring him home and put him to bed. He has done this before and his gun is only a cap pistol. Besides, he was a hero in the war.

The Flying Garcias

My sister Mary Cucha
was the first of the Garcias to fly.
I would see her above my crib
her arms stretched out,
light bristling in her curly hair.
When I could speak I asked my mother
where Mary Cucha had gone. "In the sky,"
she would answer, "your sister caught
un susto from something dark in the street
and flew away to the sky."
I spent my first years looking out the window,
paying special attention to the clouds—
the wavy ones, the ones with curly hair.

It was Inez that flew next. Balancing
along the rooftops of the neighborhood
she seemed to disappear.
I looked for her but couldn't see anything.
"It is because of her dress," Memo said.
"It's the same color as the sky,
blue with little white lines
that could be mistaken for fish scale
or buttermilk clouds, and the white carnation
she was wearing, that could be a cumulus."

My brother John said, "This family
is getting a bad reputation. If we are going
to fly, let's do it right."
I knew he was serious because he was wearing
his aviator cap and white silk scarf.
And so we flew, or rather, I, as the youngest
flew between my brothers.
Flew over *oh*s and *ah*s of upturned faces,
over the screams and squeals of beautiful women.

They are old now and have retired.
I am almost old, but I still fly.
People think I'm brave because I fly alone.
But I admit—I am afraid.
I don't like to fly alone. And I miss the slap,
the reassuring slap of my palms against the forearms
of my brother Memo, against the forearms of my brother John.

The Real Jesse James

I am the real Jesse James. I didn't die from a bullet in the back. I didn't die. I don't think so. Sometimes I'm watching my life like a movie. Sometimes I'm in the movie looking out.

~

I saw my first wife at the 1900 World's Fair. She was with her new husband, Howard, an old friend of hers who never liked me anyway. I grabbed her wrist. She looked right in my face and didn't recognize me. Howard said, "Well, well, ghosts do come back, don't they?"

~

Now I live alone. Gave up trying to prove anything. Just do my job in a shoe store. One day this lovely lady is sitting there.
"Can I help you?"
"I know who you are," she says, pointing to a book of old Western photographs on her lap. Her name is Molly and she believes in me. I almost feel like my old self again. Might even rob a bank or two.
I round up a few surviving members of the old gang and a sheriff who used to chase us. We put on a play. Not as ourselves. We don't need to convince anyone. It's a cowboy story. Toward the end I cross the stage wearing a chartreuse dress. The sheriff shoots his gun in the air and stares expectantly at the sky.
I am watching the play now with the feeling that in a moment I will understand everything. But I can't hear the dialogue. Some teenagers in the back are laughing. If those punks only knew who I really was . . . in the old days . . .

~

Molly and I are in the kitchen, about to enter the living room, where a crew from a national television show is waiting to interview us. They provided our wardrobe. A red skirt for Molly with fringes, plastic cowboy boots. For me: a multicolored shirt that looks more Hawaiian than Western, a red kerchief and a black hat that sits on top of my ears. I don't want to stand in front of a bored TV crew in these outfits. But Molly insists. This may be our last chance to prove that I am the real Jesse James. I am. I am the real Jesse James.

Wide Awake at 3:30 A.M.

As the luckiest man in Iraq
runs across a bridge,
does he know he is caught in the cross hairs
of a television camera mounted on a bomb?
He leaps to safety while the jet,
already gone, roars in his ears
and the bridge silently explodes.
Reporters at the briefing chuckle
at his narrow escape—
how he leaps just in time
to avoid the commercial for adult diapers.
We see him again, but this time
he is just a teaser for the eleven o'clock news.

I thought of him while I lay wide awake at 3:30 A.M.
I also thought about the man hanging by his wrists
in a playground, waving like a rag doll
in a wind of machine-gun bullets.
Thought not so much of him, but of the way
we see his execution for just a moment
and then some American teenagers
striding at night through an alley
in new jeans, which for some reason
are skillfully designed to appear old and ragged.
It is an industrial part of town—
warehouses, chain link fences.
It's a wet night, and they are sashaying
to music that pulses out of the ghettoblaster
one young man balances on his shoulder.
They are laughing, playfully pushing each other
into puddles and through steam that rises from manhole covers.

The Experts, the Man in the Street, the Crowd

Where do they find them, those exeprts
who appear on talk shows and the evening news
whenever we go to war? Retired generals
snatched up by helicopters from golf courses in Arizona?
Middle East scholars, old China hands?
They point to a map or place toy tanks
on papier-mâché fields. They fidget with their glasses.
They are not used to wearing glasses.
Nor do they wear their hair in that windblown,
absent-minded-professor manner. And those distinguished
gray temples were sprayed on by the makeup department . . .

I was selected once to be an expert,
but when I got to the studio
they said I was too short. Too dark.
And the wig kept sliding off.
So they used me as a man in the street.
He comes on a couple of commercials after the expert,
and gets to wear his own clothes.

Behind the man in the street is the crowd.
You think that there are many of them, but actually
it takes very few people to make a crowd.
You can't see the attendants standing behind and off to the side
with the rope. They leave it slack for a milling crowd.
Pull it tight to make the crowd seem larger, angrier.
I don't mind the experts or the man in the street so much,
but the crowd frightens me. I know you won't believe me,
but I think there is only one crowd
that moves from place to place—the same crowd
you can see in photographs that go back
to the very beginnings of photography—those tight smiles
at the company picnics and Fourth of July parades,
those flickering faces and dark eyes reflecting fire.

The Contras

If you go about the city, watch out for the Contras.
They are easy to spot.
They paint their bodies black on one side,
white on the other.
The black portion has white dots.
The white, black dots.
Of course, they are draped with weapons—
necklaces of bullets, knives protruding from their hair.
They have been known to shoot a waiter
for bringing the check too soon.
They have no leaders and belong to no faction.
If stopped by them, do not offer money or sex,
cameras, or plead for your life.
They follow the law of opposites.
Washing their hands in mud, saying good-bye
when they meet, hello as they leave,
driving their cars only in reverse.
Once, when I was stopped, I begged them to kill me.
This amused them and they cried—
cried so hard they let me go.

Roustabout

I had always wanted to make love to a woman
who could touch herself anywhere with the tip of her tongue,
and it seemed part of the act when the strongman
kicked the door in, and chased me halfheartedly
out the window and around the trailer.

When we stopped to catch our breath I tried to leave
but he begged me to stay and listen to his complaints.
"I'm tired," he said, "of holding her upside down
in front of the mirror."
"But it's all mirrors in the circus," I said,
"one mirror facing another, each containing the illusion
of a hallway that stretches into infinity."

Sandro and I have become friends. We stand arm in arm
while Sally, the contortionist, rides the elephant's neck,
waving to the audience as her hips pump back and forth.

What we like best is breaking down the big top.
We untie the last guidelines and run,
stop, and turn to watch the tent collapse into itself
like an explosion in reverse and slow motion.
What we like best is arriving at a new town in darkness,
the smell of strong black coffee, the rhythmic pounding
of a circle of men swinging sledgehammers over a stake at dawn.

The Story of Keys

If you would give me
the key to your house
I would think of it
as a one-dimensional
mountain range.
I would hold it up
to the sky
and study how clouds
drink in its valleys.
Think of it
as a tiny file
that cuts through
vertical shadows.
The door of your house
would be a rectangle of light

that shuts behind me
trapping the moon
by the coattails.
I would no longer need
the twisted path
that brought me to you.
It would disappear
along with the forest
that popped up
on springs and hinges.
And the stagehands
and roadies of my dreams
could put away their props—
cups, pools, musical perfumes
darker than your hair.

Entering for the first time
would be as if I never left.
And I would tell you
the story of keys.
They were made long before
the invention of doors.
Although no one knew their function,
wise men suspected their importance.
Carefully, they would place them
into the cracks of tree bark and twist.

Anything can be a key: a piece of wire,
a safety pin, laughter.

Swinging from the Moon on a Bosun's Chair

When he enters the house
to unstick the windows
and use the bathroom,
the painter can't help himself—
he digs through a hamper
finds her silk panties
and inhales the salty
sweetness of a sea breeze
passing over a field
of wild fennel.

He would like her
to find him asleep
in the bathtub
when she comes home at night,
to kneel and pick
the paint flecks
off the hair on his chest.
He would tell her how some insects
seem fatally attracted
to wet paint.

He would like to see her
on his stepladder
pointing out the holidays
on the ceiling—to see
her dried menstrual blood
on his thigh, the color
of red oxide primer.

Will she still love him
when it rains and he sits
in the kitchen all morning
scanning the want ads?

When he comes stumbling home,
slightly drunk,
swaying like a ladder
in his crusted overalls?

Back at work
he is on his knees
in a lilac bush.
His hand in a painter's mitt,
he dips it in clear water seal
and strokes the new cedar fence.
It is like her skin, dark and fragrant.

Delicately

She undresses
in a rectangle
of starlight
like the unfolding
of lost papyri.

Even the willow
in the backyard
has an attack
of genuflections.

Her skin contains
certain sequences
that dissolve
at the mere suggestion
that darkness
has weight.

She likes the way
he turns a radio knob—
delicately,
like a safecracker
who has sandpapered
his fingertips.

Brief Entanglements

Two dogs stuck together. The male lifts one leg
then the other over the bitch's back.
Still stuck, they face opposite directions.
As each tries to run, they spin, all eight legs
a circular blur, into the path of a speeding car.
Just as it's about to hit they break apart.

The car is driven by a couple
late to their own wedding
who were trapped in a traffic jam
where they sat without speaking,
occasionally slapping each other
like puppets in a play.

I'm on the bike path, my ten-speed
meshed with a young woman's mountain bike,
my hand on her bare thigh. I cried out
when her handlebars locked into mine
as she was trying to pass. She remains
silent, calm, as we fly along
like insects tangled in midair.
She wrestles us apart and speeds ahead.

I slow to a wobbly stop. The dogs run off in opposite directions.
The bride and groom will acquire a certain fame
for their skill at holding one kiss
as they drift through a car wash like divers sharing air.
I am leaning on one foot, almost tipped over.
The young woman rides high on the pedals
as she speeds away. Turning her head back
over her shoulder she calls out, "Sorry!"
I am sorry too. My palm tingles with an afterimage—
something smooth, muscular, yet incredibly soft.

Hôtel des Grandes Écoles

The window across from the bed,
like everything else in Paris
this jet-lagged, water-logged day,
is a little crooked. On my eyelids
it is an orange rectangle that seems to float,
smaller and smaller into darkness.
Jerking in and out of sleep
I slip off the edge of a precipice
that turns out to be a ledge
just three feet off the ground.
But it takes so long to fall
I hear myself crash
like someone slamming a piano shut,
far, very far away.
All I know of Paris is the rain—
and this room with its pink-and-white wallpaper
where eighteenth-century lovers
exchange flowers and scented notes.
Even from this distance
I can hear the song
the school children of Paris
sing beneath our window.
I am confused enough to think
that I wrote it for you.
Confused enough to think
we have slipped back a few centuries—
that I hear the rattle of carriages
and horses clip-clopping over cobblestones.
I did not want to come here
because caddis flies large as thumbnails
were due to hatch at a certain lake I know.
You insisted that I see the sky over Notre Dame.
I know there is a rumor going around—

that we are an unlikely amalgam
of fire and ice under high pressure.
They say we have come to Paris
to settle a running argument about clouds.

After the Métro Has Closed

The famous poets of Paris
have been promoted to statues
that turn to greet us
and point the way,
their hands darker
than the overcast sky
this late hour.
Or is it just that we
are slightly drunk,
wobbling our way home
with all the other couples
who must walk
after the métro has closed?
All of us kissing
like finalists
in a look-alike contest
of that classic photograph by Doisneau.

We pause on the New Bridge
that is hundreds of years old,
stare into black water,
pools of yellow light.
Trying to show you
what I learned today
I place the fingertips
of my right hand
against the fingertips
of your right hand.
This is how you make a cathedral.
Even the blind man
at the Musée Rodin, who,
with his hand on his father's shoulder
seemed to float through the room,
could see that.

Espresso this afternoon
on the Place de la Contrescarpe.
What a neighborhood!
The street musicians proved it,
and let us take a picture
to show the folks back home—
Sidney Bechet is alive and well in Paris.

Turn poets, we are turning too,
like you our hands are made of stone—
that is why we pass through the buildings so easily,
why we shall sleep soundly tonight, curled up in a giant hand.

Los Amantes

I play marimba on your rib cage
while you whistle through my thighbone.
We click clack up down escalators.
You rattle around me
taking tiny elegant steps,
whisking your skirt from side to side
as if to fan the flames
my feet stamp out.
We rub our pelvises together,
shilly-shally through lingerie
locking our bones in a romantic puzzle,
my teeth clenched to your ankle,
your hips around my neck.
Who can say this was a man
and this was a woman?
My bones love your bones.
And when I am rich enough to buy skin for you,
I will stretch it over your bones
like paper over a kite.
What a pair we will make,
strolling the avenue in the evening—
me in top hat and tails.
You with your skeleton of blue fox
slung carelessly over one shoulder.

Hiding Out

Bart lay back with his
potency established,
lit a cigarette
and stared at the ceiling
where he saw shadows forming
in the shapes of Greek sentences,
which was odd
because he didn't know any Greek.

The ventriloquist dummies
sat on the windowsill
in their perpetual silence.
One of them reminded him
of a talk show host
he had once considered murdering
because he could not get
the man's flat, nasal, whiny voice
out of his head.

Annie lay next to him feeling out of sorts,
confused, as if she had just crashed through the ceiling
and landed in a pile of blankets, sheets, magazines,
pillows, broken lathe and plaster.

She had an urge to ask him to do something outrageous,
so she sat up on the edge of the bed
and started putting on her nylons—
he could never refuse her
when she was putting on her nylons.
Something like—rob a bank
disguised as a blind man,
steal me a puppy.

The shadows, blending
with cigarette smoke, became winged demons,
protectors of some obscure nation,
who could shoot fire out of their mouths.
They tumbled across the ceiling
as if they were escaping
to the other side of the world.

The Detective Gone Bad

"Guns and ammunition," she said to him after they became lovers, "that's us." He began to understand why each gentleman caller was scrutinized by the police.

After several months of robberies and flights through different states, they quarreled, and took off in separate cars in different directions. Abruptly, at the same instant, the cars veered around as if irresistibly drawn together and almost collided.

In that moment she knew he wanted to extinguish a crown of matches from her head one by one with his .45, while she stood in front of a spinning target in her cowgirl outfit. He knew that he would abandon everything for her—his office, friends, and family.

These same friends and family that would one day pursue both of them through the swamps, that would return to her house and join the neighbors with the intention of burning it down.

But they could not bring themselves to do it. They were afraid of her collection of ventriloquist dummies, the way they stared silently from each window.

Hotel Boston

"Three A.M.," the note said,
"Ask for Ralph, the security guard."
But there was no Ralph,
only a gate pretending to be locked
that swung open, too easily it seemed,
at his touch. The slats of the freight elevator
crossed his face in flashing shadows
as he rode it to the third floor.
It was a mannequin factory
and the torsos hung upside down
in long rows—each face,
with its slight sophisticated smile,
a perfect copy of the next.
The hips and legs piled in a corner
made him think of a giant erector set.

He called out, "Where are you, doll?"
but received no answer.
Why did she always pick these places—
unfinished freeway ramps,
abandoned amusement parks and hobo jungles?
Why did she—or was it his idea—insist
on their always meeting each other
for the first time as if they were strangers?
The fortune-teller had warned him
about ladies who look good in black or red,
who like to dance by themselves
to Stravinsky's "Rite of Spring"
while he sat smoking at a nightclub table
improvised out of five-gallon cans and scrap wood.

If this were a movie a switch would be thrown
and the mannequins would roll before him
on a conveyor belt. Or he would hear a faint sound

and realize that one of the hairless, naked figures
was breathing. But it wasn't a movie.
And when he ground his cigarette out,
he noticed the familiar crumpled shape
of one of her notes. "Caracas," it said,
"Hotel Boston." He knew it well. The mirrored hallway
that multiplied their images as they strode
toward the desk like a regiment marching in perfect step.
They would be laughing, and their laughter would echo, rising
and falling in waves like the laughter of a huge crowd.

No Quarrels Today

Mother carried a washbasin
into the bathroom and placed it in the bathtub.
She wrapped her apron around her waist
like she meant business, tied a bandanna on her head,
and crossed herself like a bullfighter
before a shrine of the Virgin. We knew we had to be careful
because this was New Year's Eve,
the day she made tamales
and, as she warned us every year,
if there was a harsh word in the house,
the tamales would not be good.

When Teresa locked herself in the car
and her husband punched the windshield,
the tamales were no good.
The time I made fun of my niece
because she was cross-eyed, and I scared my sister
by standing like a zombie in her closet,
the tamales were no good.
When Titi Rosa took a swing at Guillermo
with her cane, when everyone called Johnny a drunk
because he fell asleep beneath the Christmas tree
with his head in the *nacimiento*, and Richie
was telling each guest that my mother missed
while trying to spit in the bathtub and it landed in the *masa*,
the tamales were no good.

Every year we laughed, but not too loud,
Nobody crossed my mother. My older brother,
a grown man with a wife and children,
had to come to her and beg forgiveness on his knees.
Not a figure of speech, but on his knees.
If you asked her to throw the *cartas*
you had better be prepared for the truth.

Once she looked up from the ace of spades
and told Vicente, "Go home, get your house in order,"
and he was dead in a week.
When she said to Rachel, who was poor as a mouse,
"You will take a trip across the ocean and fall in love on the ship,"
Rachel went straight to the beauty parlor.

That is why we tiptoed around and said please and excuse me,
why we did not make jokes about the saints
or sit in the dark staring in the mirror hoping to see the devil.
Why at one in the morning the party got quiet
when we carried out two steaming tins from the kitchen,
each with one hundred tamales, some with chicken, chile,
and two olives, some sweet with honey and corn.
It was New Year's and my sister Inez's birthday
and even strangers who came to our party by mistake
came back every year. And everyone sitting around our house,
from the *sala* to the *cucurucho*, eating Cuka's famous tamales,
knew we had behaved ourselves, at least for one day,
because the tamales were good.

Waiting in a Parked Car

As when some folk song slowly starts out,
Baltic perhaps, one two, one two, one two
so slowly, so slow, the words based
on a famous poem by someone
who admired the feminine beauty
of the hills of the motherland,
the streams flowing between their clefts,
the wheat neatly bound in sheaves,
a peasant girl and lad asleep in a haystack—
or as when an accordion builds slowly faster
and faster to shouts of *Hey! Hey!*
to hand clapping, thigh slapping, to piercing whistles
that stab the melody and make the dancers
(when you hear music there are dancers)
excited, taking shorter and shorter,
faster and faster steps
in a measured madness—
and I am thinking: surely, they will fall
down crazy when the song stops—

as when some folk song
is heard on the car radio
while I sit waiting for my stepdaughter
to come out from her therapy appointment,
while I sit admiring the muscular legs of a woman
who appears to be on her way to work, the way
they bulge, almost leaping out of the black skirt
that is tight around her hips, it all makes me think
that I must live in at least two worlds,
one of them crowded with a colorful
blur of dancers spinning in national costumes.
But now I see my lovely stepdaughter coming toward me
in the rearview mirror. The song has ended,
exposing naked silence and afternoon sunlight,

chunky, circular, crazed as Van Gogh sunlight.
It is time for the peasant girl and lad to wake and join the others
sweating in the dusty field. They look so perfectly happy
wrapped up in the hay that holds them in the grasp of the same dream.
No one, not their fellow workers,
not the dancers, not I, has the heart to wake them.

Open Letter to My Friends

Today I learned that black smoke glowing red
at its base is a new fire. White means
the firemen are there with ropes of water.
Large flakes of ash drift by my window, dark gray
with a fringe of white, like expensive lettuce
or the edge of surf seen from an airplane.

Down below, whole families run by my front gate
carrying shopping bags full of shoes. Everything
anyone ever wanted is free. Gang members
who live across the street are more methodical,
military in their short haircuts, white T-shirts
and black baggy pants. They stride two by two
out of the alley and into their cars, returning later
with trunks full of electronic equipment.

I am becoming a connoisseur of night sounds:
the distant chatter of automatic rifles,
the popping of a .22, a car alarm.
I can tell the difference between the whoosh
of Molotov cocktails and the rip a shotgun
makes in the air. This city manufactures
its own clouds—solid, symmetrical, metallic.
they press against the sky from horizon to horizon
propped up by twirling pylons.

The streets are lined with trees bursting with purple blossoms.
But you probably don't believe me—accustomed to my lies,
you never believe me when I tell the truth.

72

The Wild Boy and His Dog

"Ruff," he would call to him,
"Ruff, Ruff, come and watch me throw rocks
at the children!" The dog would come running
and bark while the boy threw rocks at the children
who were on their way to school.
He would shake his favorite stick at them,
and screech hard words down from the hill.

Long ago, when the boy and the children
were babies, he had led them
away from the nursery into the hospital basement.
He showed them how to drink from puddles under the pipes,
how to steal food at night from the kitchen.
Together they listened to the metal birds
that taught them a language
of bang and chirp and chug and creak and hiss.
There they played, until grown-ups came crashing
through barricades of sheet rock and sawhorses.

After the boy escaped from the big box,
the grown-ups gave up trying to catch him.
It was Ruff who brought him the food they left
each day at the foot of the hill.
Sometimes the boy and his dog
would creep down in the darkness
and see how the houses were growing in rows,
how they seemed to flicker with blue light as they slept.
Ruff and the boy crept close to the walls
and listened, even peered in the windows.
The boy could talk to Ruff
and knew some of the grown-ups' words—
like birthday meant blow on fire.
But he was forgetting how to talk to the machines
that squawked and pecked at the earth in the fields below.

The Book of Forgetting

Hearing her humming to herself
while he lay on the bed with his eyes closed
he thought she was in his arms.
He opened his eyes and was surprised
to see her standing across the room.

That night a priest and a rabbi
entered both their dreams.
The priest, Father Lapanzo, had a tiny mirror
that had survived the flood. Rabbi Elisha
had a book that made you forget things.

They had traveled together looking for these two
for a long time. It seems there had been some mixup.
The priest tried to catch their attention
by holding the mirror to the sun.
But there was no sun in either of their dreams.

"Let me handle it," said the rabbi,
and he began to read backwards
from the book of forgetting.
But it was too late, the man had rolled over
which was a signal for the woman to roll over.
They both woke at the same moment and remembered
they had forgotten something important.

About the Author

RICHARD GARCIA was born in 1941 in San Francisco. A first-generation American (his father was from Puerto Rico, his mother from Mexico), Garcia grew up "in a house without books," he writes, "except for one on the meanings of dreams." He is also the author of *Selected Poetry* and a bilingual children's book, *My Aunt Otilia's Spirits*. He has received a fellowship from the National Endowment for the Arts and four fellowships from the California Arts Council, three as poet-in-residence at the Long Beach Museum of Art. He is currently poet-in-residence at Childrens Hospital Los Angeles in a program sponsored by the Mark Taper Foundation.

Pitt Poetry Series

Ed Ochester, General Editor